What son

"…reflect[s] the hesitation, confusion, messiness, and satisfaction involved in living a full life…"

—Karen Gilden

"…a satisfying read…Your reflections led me on a process of guided introspection…I was engaged with your narrative in a way that required me to seek answers for myself."

—Gerry Bertsch

"…a wonderful addition to your oeuvre!"

—Linda Chaplik

"…that feeling of sharing breaks through, and it's then that I feel awed about what I'm reading."

—Bob Buckley

"…represents a sweeping view of prominent topics and events in the mid-to-late 20th century and into the early 21st century…issues as experienced by a woman who observes them through her professional and personal roles in American society."

—Cynthia Bertsch

"You have a lot of wisdom to share."

—Kathleen Haley

How Much Is Enough?

a meander of memoir essays

Sally Petersen

Also by Sally Petersen

Remembrances: Class of 1950,
Holdrege High School
(limited edition)

The Real American Dream: Creating Independence
And Running a One-Person Business

Miniatures
(chapbook)

Tea Pie, Love and Reality:
A Collection of Memoir Essays

I May Never Get to Petra:
A Second Collection of Memoir Essays

ISBN: 979-8-9859679-0-6

Cover and book design: Anita Jones, Another Jones Graphics

ꝗP
Petersen Publications
Sally@PetersenPublications.com

Contents

Acknowledgements

A solitary person, alone with her thoughts, doesn't write a book, although that's usually where it begins. Read the acknowledgements page of any book and you will find lengthy lists of people who helped.

If, as some of us believe, making a book is like having a baby, the analogy holds: the idea is the author's, the responsibility for accuracy, integrity and hard work is the author's but without a support system, she wouldn't make it. Clarifying ideas by bouncing them off other people, encouragement, criticism, and suggestions (all valuable commodities) come from others.

I also want to thank Anita Jones of Another Jones Graphics in Missoula, Montana. She keeps trying to retire, and Jim and I keep writing books. So Anita graciously produces another cover, another table of contents and deals with another printer.

So, you are holding another baby in your hands, and here are the people without whom I couldn't have done it. The writers support group of Martha Ragland, Glennis McNeal, Karen Gilden, Diane Lund, Kim Cook, Jim Petersen. The wonderful beta readers who helped clean up the baby before it went out into the world: Gerry and Cynthia Bertsch, Bob Buckley, Wally and Sandy Carey, Linda Chaplik, Allan Charsha-May, Karen Gilden, Kathleen Haley, Nan Narboe, Lisa Marie Petersen and Nicole Petersen.

Dear Jim, stalwart supporter that he is, deserves a separate word. Thank you, my love.

About the Author

Sally Petersen, a native of Nebraska, lives in Portland, Oregon, where mountains and giant fir trees obscure her longed-for view of the horizon. She occasionally escapes to the nearby Pacific Ocean and can be observed staring out to sea.

A friend says Sally "always rounds up."

Another, in a discussion about wearing black to a book reading, glances over and nods, "Oh, that's right. You wear color."

Seeking the horizon, rounding up, choosing color, enjoying quirkiness and appreciating the moments of flat-out beauty in a mundane life…Sally does those things in life and in her writing.

There's other stuff—she's been a journalist, a business owner, a neighborhood organizer, a columnist, a consultant. She's a wife, a mother, a grandmother, a great grandmother. All these roles, all these different lives and a love of meandering led to *How Much Is Enough?*

Introduction

The Pilot Light

The question How much is enough? comes to me often these days, post-pandemic, mid-Ukraine-angst, approaching another birthday with a zero at the end.

Life has been good to me and I wouldn't *have* to do anything. My generation drew the long straw. Many of us remaining from the long-ago Silent Generation are solvent and healthy. We could coast along, playing bridge or golf, summering north, wintering south. We could *play* out our days. Some do, happily. Why don't I?

Well, because I can't.

A small urge somewhere inside says, *Do More. Keep at it. What you've done is not enough. You have more to do.*

As a self-deprecating daughter of the Nebraska plains, I have resisted calling this urge anything as lofty as "creativity." Instead, I think in terms of "tasks," and "projects." Creativity seemed like the province of long-haired painters in Paris, Hemingway in Havana, or writers flourishing in the hot-box of sunny LA.

But I also understand that I love beginning to think about something that doesn't exist, and then making it happen. Lately I've reluctantly come to see it as my calling, my work in life. I've tiptoed into the idea that this even may be the creative urge, identifiable, nameable, and time for me to own.

This urge in me is not huge. It's like a fire that flickers quietly sometimes, grows bigger and demands to be fed at other times, but seems never to go out. Maybe we could think of it as a pilot light.

This pilot light tells me I'm not happy unless engaged in an overarching, stretching project. A task bigger than I can do easily. Something requiring initiation, thought, preparation and effort. A project that makes me question whether I really can do it well, that has dry days with no output as well as delirious moments in the zone.

I think of my examples: having a baby, starting a business, writing a book, climbing a glacier mountain. I need an activity like that. Without it, I get cranky, stubborn, suspicious, flabby in mind and body.

However, I am not "driven." I spend a lot of time doing "nothing"¬—reading, staring out the window, making soup.

In most ways my life has been easy; privileged in the ways that count. I've always understood that being a blue-eyed blonde in the white person's world of Nebraska, where the narrative was clear, put me in an environment where I could aspire despite being female. Plus being confident in your ability to figure things out gives one an edge in life, and I've always felt I could figure out pretty much anything. (Unless it's math-based.)

I don't feel especially loveable, so in later years it has come as a surprise when I am loved. Childhood was different. Love began with my parents. I didn't mind living up to their expectations, probably because I could meet them with relative ease. I was smart; they were appreciative. People around me also appreciated and nurtured me—in my home, in the Presbyterian church we belonged to, aunts and uncles, teachers in the good schools America had in the 1940s and '50s, friends of all ages in a small town.

I came to understand that I could do well without having to work *really* hard. I've never had a huge drive to excel beyond a certain point. That point hovers around a B plus or an A minus. That's been enough. I did not strive for A plus. I was not valedictorian of my small high school; I was neither a Phi Beta Kappa in college, nor first on any campus list of achievers. But I did have successes, and they were not insignificant. I earned them not to make up for something or to fill a hole in me. I worked in response to the pilot light.

I did and still do push myself, responding in fits and starts to that unnameable something that spurs people to exploration and new work.

However, I question it now, and that's what kicked off this book.

It's the question I live with—what do I understand of the pilot light at this stage of life? Am I still living up to what my parents wanted decades after their deaths? Do I feel obligated to use my above-average good fortune? Do I have a desire to give back? After all, I am of the generation that grew up hearing "from those to whom much is given, much will be required."

Or am I simply having fun? Is the desire to know more and do more simply who I am, my nature supported by a confidence-building youth and some luck.

As I slow down, I find myself saying "No" with increasing frequency. As a younger woman, I said "no" occasionally. After all, I'm an introvert surrounded by active, energetic people who like activity. Me? I like to be alone, to read, to observe. But often my "no" meant nothing. Over the years

I've been talked into doing things. Like climbing Mt. Hood, traveling to South Africa, taking newly-created jobs no one had done before.

Now, people tend to take me at my word, and I revel in saying, "no."

Part of saying "no" is this come-and-go feeling I've alluded to—that somehow I've done enough. That I can do what I *want*, not what I *should*.

An issue arises though—enough of what? What does "enough" apply to? Enough of exercising, eating sensibly, participating in groups where I will have little to no impact? Enough travel, which is not fun anymore with a world-wide pandemic still on the loose and the officious TSA apparently in place forever?

Another aspect of the question puzzles me: Is my desire to do less, to say "enough," a sign of maturity? Or childishness?

The case for maturity argues that aging is for contemplation, for attending to spiritual matters, for consolidating and enjoying the wisdom it took so long to acquire. This might mean saying no to old responsibilities and outdated ideas of what's necessary. It could mean turning away from activities and people who don't nourish us. Here in the Pacific Northwest, it can mean spending more time enjoying our abundant natural surroundings without having to "do" anything.

The other case—that it's a sign of childishness—is the sneaking suspicion that screwing up your face, pounding your fists, and screaming "no!" is reminiscent of a two-year-old who has just learned to assert herself.

But learning to say no, to establish boundaries, is a necessary stage for children—what if it is for those of us who are aging as well? What if our job now is to get rid of the old commitments that cluster around following other people's expectations? To think for ourselves.

We have few good role models for becoming old. Our culture dislikes even the words—old, aging, So, what if our task is to use the creative urge, our pilot lights, to make a template for becoming our authentic, congruent, wise selves? We might leave the next generation a different template. One that bypasses both Botox and boredom.

Daily I'm reminded that being "old," is different from being "really old." Really old means anything over the mid-80s. So, for me, this issue comes into play with increasing seriousness. Should I keep pushing myself? Why? Why not?

The pieces that follow are the results of spending time fooling around with those questions. Some are frivolous—after all, who cares if I still wear Levi's or what I cook? Some are practical. Some go deeper.

Almost daily I wrestle with these "enough" questions.

What about continuing to exercise, to remain healthy? Aerobic exercise will keep oxygen flowing to my brain and help with neural plasticity. Do I care? I actually will be quite content to leave this beat-up old world for younger people to worry about. Is there a time limit on the "it's good for you" stuff of life? On pushing yourself?

What about the big project? Is it actually creativity that needs to be honored? Or just habit? Without a book to write would I really become dopey and stagnant? Or would I learn to love watching the grass grow?

I talk to myself about this. I ask why roll the dice again? Why subject yourself to possible failure when your right shoulder aches from using the track pad, your eyes sting from monitor flare, and an entertaining mystery book awaits by the fire in the living room?

Ahh, I think. Here's the answer in your bachelor-button blue eyes, your direct gaze. This is the real you, isn't it? The seeker. The striver. The woman whose mantra is "never say die, say damn."

Okay, I'll drink to that. Come along. We'll sip Ouzo, that excellent Greek aperitif. Like it, we'll turn white in response to the ice of old age, but keep our flavor and kicks.

Part One

Levi's—Enough?

In the 1940s, Levi's denim was stiff and dark. A pair of pants turned wash water blue for many washings. They shrank. That meant buying at least one size too big and washing two or three times before wearing them. It wasn't cool to wear new-looking Levi's, even then.

The ubiquitous blue pants basically were clothing for male farmers, ranchers and cowboys. They didn't fit "traditional" female shapes. The hips were too tight, waists too big, legs too long. So, we guessed at sizes, washed to shrink and bought belts to shape them a little.

In our town on the plains of Nebraska girls couldn't wear any kind of trousers to school—even when outside temperatures sank below zero and snow whipped past on blizzard winds. By my senior year we had worn the principal down with requests and complaints, and were allowed to wear jeans under our skirts to school in the winter. But once we got there, we had to take them off and stash them in our lockers for the day.

Over the next sixty years, Levi's modified their pants to fit people with thighs. They replaced buttons with zippers. As stretch materials improved, Levi's used them. Dark blue denim never went away, but black, gray and light blue joined the crowd. Now we have boot cuts and straight-legs, slim cut and fulsome (also known as mom jeans), heavy or light weight, worn-out knees and holes in strange places—something for everyone.

I embraced the ill-fitting but long-lasting cowboy-style of the '40s. Seventy-five years later, I'm still wearing the same brand. They're now fashionably slim and fitting very well, thank you.

But some days I wonder if a woman at ninety still should be wearing Levi's. Age-appropriate? Well, they are comfortable, incredibly long-lasting and rain-repellant enough for most days in an Oregon winter.

Still, how many years of Levi's are enough?

Which brings me to…

The Body

I've had a love-hate relationship with my body for most of my life, as have many women my age. (Okay, many women of almost any age…)

Females of our species have been judged on appearance from the moment we arrived. If we were lucky—that is if we showed up whole and healthy—our parents and friends cooed, "What a pretty baby!" We grew up understanding that we'd always be judged on our looks and shape first, while any other attributes would come second. (Our brothers might have heard, "What a strong little guy!")

When we were young, we didn't know about airbrushing and therefore couldn't realize that the bodies we saw in ads were about as real as Popeye. Looking at them, many of us would have preferred to resemble a teen-age boy. Y'know, tall and slim, tiny hips, no thighs…the model thing. That was the way women "should" look.

For me, however, no amount of wishing made that happen, so eventually, like most people, I learned to work with what I had.

In addition to their cosmetic aspects, bodies are like automobiles issued to us at birth. We use them to get around and they need maintenance.

It's this maintenance that annoys me. To continue the mechanical model, I want my appliances—washing machines, dishwashers, computers and cars—to function flawlessly all the time. I don't want to have to fiddle with them; I'm not a tinkerer. It's the same with my body. My natural approach to life is to move only when necessary—for instance, to get another book, to make a pb&j sandwich and pour milk to go with it, or to locate a wee dram of Scotch and a handful of cashews.

The maintenance issue surfaced early—near the end of my college career. I was editing the university newspaper, studying for finals, preparing for a wedding, and participating in the end-of-year activities of social and campus activity groups. Plus partying pretty hard.

When I began to have erratic episodes of blacking out, part of the preventive prescription was to exercise, also hard. "If you're not sweating," my doctor said, "You're not doing enough." In response, my fiancé and I added one more activity to the already exhausting list. We rented bikes and pedaled through springtime parks in Lincoln, Nebraska, exercising away the excess tension.

Body maintenance next popped up when, after I indulged in a spectacular weight gain, my first daughter was delivered. While she needed to gain weight, I needed to lose it to handle motherhood. Thus exercise came back into my life. This regimen repeated twice with other daughters.

Sometimes workouts were solitary. Other times I was watched by a quizzical cat or a younger daughter who thought floor exercises were mom playing with her. Often I enrolled in structured classes. One instructor was dubbed "the young Nazi," but she got me to run a nine-minute mile.

In each case, alone or in a group, as soon as I became satisfied with results I stopped.

Despite my best efforts I continued to age. During my corporate years, bursitis showed up and required remedial exercise. Then a cranky gallbladder followed a useless uterus into hospital incinerators. Surgery requires that at some point you begin to exercise its effects away. So again, I began the routine. This time I joined a health club and dutifully hoisted dumbbells and bent this way and that.

Retirement seemed great until I discovered to my surprise that if I didn't move—often—I hurt. *Use it* or *lose it* moved from being someone else's slogan to being my reality.

So, I'm back at it with a personal trainer.

"What do you want?" he asks.

"To stay flexible and gain strength." So now he issues me "homework."

I guess this is forever. No "enough" here.

Maybe I should have come to terms with this issue earlier. But I'm still caught by surprise that I wasn't an auto with an automatic lifetime lube in my warranty.

Cooking: Evolution

I didn't learn to cook in my mother's kitchen. I was relegated to the unvarying role of helper. Here she is, speaking to me:

"Chop the onions and tomatoes."

"Stir this for ten minutes or until it thickens."

"Measure one and a half cups of flour into this bowl. Add a pinch of salt and get me three eggs."

"Flour the glass and cut the biscuit dough. Then put them on the cookie sheet."

"Go outside and get a handful of little green onions from where your dad planted them in the tulip bed. They should be up by now."

"Wash the quart jars—we're canning peaches today."

Some instructions had three or four parts, but none involved teaching me to produce an end product. Except for fudge. And ice cream.

After four years of university, studying political science, history, literature and newspapering, it occurred to me that soon I'd be married, and my lack of culinary experience might become a problem.

In the 1950s, marriage meant things I'd managed to avoid during my first twenty-one years—cleaning a house, setting up a household, and, oh, lord, stocking a kitchen and preparing three meals a day. In 1954, there was no question about whose tasks these were. Women had been sent home after helping win World War II and were expected to stay there.

I'd somehow learned to cook bacon, scramble eggs and

turn Wonder Bread into toast, even French toast in a pinch. I knew my way around a sandwich and a salad. So, I could finesse two meals. But dinner?

There at the last minute, just weeks before the wedding, I pinned my mother down and made her show me some of the easy stuff of mid-American cooking—spaghetti and meat-balls, pork chops, meat loaf, ham loaf garnished with canned pineapple slices and accompanied by whipped cream horse-radish sauce.

Did mom feel territorial about the kitchen domain where she ruled? Or was it real when she said, "You have the rest of your life to do these household things. Enjoy yourself while you can." I later realized how much those sentences betrayed an attitude about her life's work.

As it turned out, once started, cooking took hold of me. I loved its ancillary tasks of setting a beautiful—or at least clever—table, arranging flowers and candles as support actors for the meal. I took easily to the idea of combining colors and textures in food to create drama on the plate. I specialized in dinner parties for six or eight—ten max—both casual and formal.

I occasionally sought more enthusiastic teachers than my mother. In the late fifties, at the local community college, I learned to handle a chef's knife, make canapés and various complex, pretty hors d'oeuvres. In the '60s I researched and cooked Japanese food to showcase lacquered soup bowls my husband brought home from military R&R in Japan. Then, bless her heart, Julia Child wrote a book that taught me the joys of French cooking.

At another level of complexity, we camped—first alone, then with daughters—among great Douglas fir forests on mountainsides, by lakes and the sea. I designed weekend menus featuring French toast, corned beef hash topped with poached eggs, cracked crab with crusty French bread and white wine.

At the end of one beautiful warm back-packing day high in the northern Cascades I added just-picked mountain-meadow huckleberries to stream water and boiled them into syrup, then threw more huckleberries into pancakes. It was one of the most elegant meals I've ever cooked, there at 7000 feet.

Years passed. In a large home I rejoiced in my vegetable garden—three lettuces, Early Girl, cherry, and heirloom tomatoes, onions, zucchini and cucumbers. Parsley and chives tucked into the flower beds, just as my father had placed his onions among the tulips a lifetime ago in Nebraska. Entertaining now consisted of groups of twenty, forty or a hundred. Graduations, engagement parties and weddings. I had too many people in my life to justify the work of a dinner for six or eight…the perfect number for good conversation, in my estimation. But it didn't take much more effort to serve fifty, just another few people to help with serving and cleanup.

Retirement eventually took our party of two to a small condo. This prevented big gatherings, and I shared daily cooking with a retired husband who liked to fry things. We ate out often. And eureka! we found at least three apps we used to order restaurant meals delivered. Entire meals arrived, hot and good enough.

Food delivery seemed a small miracle for the days I thought about the chuck roast that needed either to be cooked or frozen along with the carrots, potatoes, and onions languishing in the hydrator drawer.

Then my husband and I rather casually decided to try whole-food, plant-based eating not too long after the great pandemic kept us confined to quarters. After making the change, we felt so much better eating that way we never looked back. The number of pot roasts I had cooked to that point turned out to be "enough."

Once again our cooking has changed and we're enjoying the challenge. Best is the "whole food" part of the system.

Although some days I wonder how many beans are enough…

卍卍卍

The Sports Fan

Girls didn't play team sports when I was in high school, a public school in Midwestern farm country in the 1940s.

Our school did have a girls basketball team—they played a half-court game—but I didn't try out. A half-court game was silly. Even in those days we knew we could do more. Besides, physical education classes had taught me I wasn't good enough. Hand-eye coordination and physical prowess didn't make the list of my better characteristics. I wasn't even good at volleyball, sort of a lowest common denominator.

Our town didn't support individual sports like tennis, and I was no good at bowling, which I regarded as beneath my dignity anyway. My young, judgmental self asked, can you even call it a sport if people playing the game are drinking beer?

So, I joined the pep club and the marching band and became a football fan.

My boyfriend Wayne played tackle, and I came to admire the strong, steady linemen of the sport. Quarterbacks and running backs are spectacular, but I loved the work of the line that made it all possible. So did the coach and players. On our winning teams, Wayne did his work at tackle so well that in the last game of our senior year they gave him the ball, opened the opposing line and sent him across to score the final touchdown.

I segued smoothly into being a sturdy University of Nebraska football fan, even though we had a terrible record my years there. I knew some of the varsity players. Several came from small towns like mine; it was not that much different from high school.

My next serious bout of fandom came on the West Coast when Portland's NBA team, the Trailblazers, cruised to a national championship in 1977. Caught up in the excitement of the whole small state, I watched and learned to appreciate their fluid grace and tenacity. I noted the hard work that changed a group of talented young men of varied backgrounds into a remarkably consistent, winning team.

Their run to the championship came shortly after my decision to change my life, to re-marry, move to a new state, shake everything up. It felt as if we were on an exciting course together.

The man I married had been a college tennis player, although he didn't play again until years later. Then, because I'm curious and kind, I became a fan of a new game. Twice a week he plays and often I hear the games recounted.

We watch this international sport on TV. I've learned to appreciate Roger Federer's balletic grace and power, the every-shot-counts ferocity of Rafa Nadal, and Serena Williams' teeth-gritting tendency to pull out of trouble. To say nothing of her ability to win the Australian Open while pregnant…Woo Hoo!

But the longest lasting of these fan sports in my life has been baseball.

The farm teams of farm teams began coming through Holdrege in the summers when I was in high school. They played under the lights at a field I couldn't locate today.

What I can locate is the peaceful memory of sitting in wooden stands, feeling that warm night on my bare arms and legs, the trim tight bodies of the young men on the field, the comforting steadiness of the game—three up, three down, change places, repeat. I loved the satisfying seventh-inning stretch and the recurring high tension of three balls, two strikes.

I tune into major league baseball somewhere towards the end of the playoffs. I want to learn the players before settling in to watch the World Series. What a ring that has, "World Series." As if it were something more than a few professional teams in the US, with their plus-one, Toronto.

I like the stories, such as the Molina brothers, those terrific catchers from the same Puerto Rican family, but mostly I relax into the visuals—a home run ball arching across a night sky, lawnmowing prowess displayed on the infield, a hands-out player sliding into second base. And the realization that until the very last, something, someone, could kick loose the slowly unfolding story and change the ending.

By the Numbers

Jim, my husband, and I joke that we've flunked retirement. In our upper 80s, we write and run a small book publishing business together. Sometimes we wonder about quitting, finding someone else to do the work. We ask ourselves, haven't we worked enough?

Age 16

I held my first real job in Nebraska as a telephone operator at the age I legally could join the workforce doing anything besides babysitting or mowing lawns.

Ages 19 to 21

During my university years, being a student reporter and then editor at the Daily Nebraskan was considered a job and came with a stipend. Summers back home meant working as replacement for vacationing telephone operators.

From 21 to 26

Six days after graduation I married Ken. Two weeks after that I began a funny little job in Omaha, telephoning people who lived on corners, assigning them a street address. When my husband entered graduate school in California in the fall, I became a "girl Friday" in the Berkeley Camp Fire Girls office. That morphed into a field director job in the Oakland office when my husband went to Korea. I trained volunteer leaders up and down the East Bay in suburban communities beginning their California growth spurt. After he returned, within six weeks I was working as a newspaper reporter in the Pacific Northwest.

From 26 to 41

After a while, I took fifteen years out of the workforce to have daughters and be a full-time mom—women did that in those days. Not that being a mom and volunteer weren't full-time jobs. Still, I managed to fit a paying job into the middle of that time during a 5-year sojourn in Iowa. As food editor for the Des Moines Register, I wrote a daily column and every six weeks, I journeyed out with a photographer and wrote front page feature stories for the life-style section. Loved that job.

Ages 41 to 67

Back in the Northwest I became a neighborhood organizer for three years. I also divorced, re-married, moved to Oregon and commuted while continuing to organize. This was followed by ten years at Tektronix, Oregon's big high-tech firm, during which time I accumulated eight job titles and a master's degree. When the corporate world added me to a layoff, I started into business as a writer, editor and desktop publisher. Self-employment lasted thirteen years. I had fun and wrote my first book.

Finally, ages 67 to 90

Since "retirement," I've written and produced two more books while my husband just finished the third edition of his book. I'm working on this, my third volume of miniature essays. He also began gainful employment in high school and has worked continuously since then, including college years.

Some days—all right, many days—we walk out of our offices and ask each other… *How much is enough?*

Hurry Up!

Older people tend to arrive places early. They don't mind waiting—for the dentist, the airplane, for the party to start. I first learned this when I sat on the board of an organization that served senior citizens. When we held a yearly appreciation gathering, we built in an extra 45 minutes to an hour before lunch to accommodate early arrivals.

I think I figured out why this happens. Many people have had a long lifetime of hurrying, and it's been enough. They'd prefer to mosey along through their preparations—perhaps a nap, then shower, change clothing, settle the dog or cat, set the TV to record a show for later, leave early, drive or be driven without hurry—get somewhere early. And wait without irritation for things to begin.

Many of these people have had long years of worrying about time. They've had to get children cleaned, clothed and out the door for school, had to be at the office or warehouse on time, needed to punch a time clock, or be there when the judge arrived or the shift changed. Some have had thirty-eight things to do before running to catch a plane. Others needed to be at school early to get the day underway before students arrived. Military people always were at someone else's mercy on timing. Analog or digital, whatever their situation, in some way the clock ruled their lives.

Those lucky enough to retire without having to find another job become free from time's tyranny. With their new freedom, many people simply will not be hurried. So they amble along, getting to places early.

Hurry up? No. They've had enough.

I'm with them. All my life, it seems, someone has been telling me to hurry up. I still remember my first natural history museum. It was in Hastings, Nebraska, a nearby city where my mother took my brother and me to get eye glasses. We spent the afternoon in the museum, eyes dilated, as lenses were ground. It was slow work, reading signs at a wildlife diorama with fuzzy sight. I wanted to absorb every word, while my younger brother and an impatient mother wanted what I considered a brisk pace. Hurry up, Sally! It became a refrain I lived with.

I was born an owl, not a lark, so school years from the upper grades through university were one long period of morning agony. At the beginning, I read by flashlight under the covers at night, as all future writers do, so morning found me grumpy and foggy. Late nights and bad mornings outlasted flashlights, morphing into late reading or studying. Hurry up, you'll be late for school was the call of all those years.

Then came years in the workforce. During them I told two husbands on many mornings, "Please don't talk to me before 10. I can get out of bed, dressed, fed and to the office, but I cannot think or carry on a conversation of any significance."

Working years, getting children to school on time years, working and children years—all time-sensitive, all with some reason for someone to say, "Hurry up, Mom. We're going to be late." From kindergarten to graduation ceremonies, from the excitement of a new job to the ennui of one about over, from a little tyke pulling at you to the necessity of showing on time for a wedding, I struggled with time. Never enough.

So, if other people are like me, at some point they've had enough of other people's timing, scheduling. They decide to go at their own slow pace, to get places early, then to sit, happily waiting for some younger person hurrying to get to them. Rushing around is in the rearview mirror.

This is a deliberate choice, made in the name of ease and calm.

We've had enough.

Books, Vinyl Records and Where They Are Now

In the mid-1970s, my former husband and I pioneered the concept of an amiable divorce. At that time, you were assumed to hate each other if you split, expected to fight in and out of court, badmouth each other to friends and children. But we rejected that concept. After all, we were Nebraskans, a species known around the world as "nice." We had been friends before marriage, studying political science, history and journalism together at the University of Nebraska.

That joint study, with its ensuing (and lasting) joint interests, gave us our only real problem in the split: books. I am irritated to this day, forty-five years later, that Ken appropriated our joint copy of Garret and Godfrey, *Europe Since 1815.* But I kept our college yearbooks, and that irritated him, too, because he had to telephone or email to ask me to look people up for the next thirty years.

When Ken died a few years ago, I could have scooped up any books I wanted since our girls' interests were different. My personal relationship with Garret and Godfrey resurfaced. When I thought to retrieve the book, it was damp and sniffy from too many years of Oregon coast weather. With a deep sigh, I trudged it to Goodwill.

Some years later, I began the downsizing that accompanies a smaller, less demanding home. The First Extinction. A quick glance showed my books accurately reflected stages in my life:

• Childhood, mine and my daughters': compilations of fairy tales and Mother Goose rhymes, *The Saggy, Baggy Elephant*, Carl Sandburg's *Rootabaga Stories*, the Ant & Bee series. What I thought of as my "war books," printed during

WWII with cheap, crackly paper, light covers, prices under 50 cents. These were the Nancy Drew mysteries—the first printed when I was a year and a half old—*Black Beauty,* the Bobbsey Twins and Outdoor Girls series and *Heidi.* I had a lovely, illustrated book of Native American tales, *Here is Alaska,* and Camp Fire Girls handbooks of several eras.

• College, texts (see Garret & Godfrey), art history, gigantic yearbooks, Arthur Koestler.

• Years of learning to be a corporate woman: *Games Mother Never Taught You* by Betty Lehan Harragan, Molloy's *Dress for Success.*

• More years of learning to be myself, so that I could negotiate the world more intentionally: *Dance of Anger* by Harriett Lerner; all Marsha Sinetar's books; *Written by Herself* and most of Jill Ker Conway; *When Women Were Priests* and others books about religion before patriarchy took over; women's biographies.

• Cookbooks: both the kind you read and the kind you cook from.

• Writing: almost everything William Zinsser wrote, Strunk & White, (still on my shelf from college), Annie Dillard, Steven King, *The Artist's Way* by Julia Cameron.

• When my parents died, I acquired my dad's falling-apart mineral and rock field guide, his field guide to birds and a few pamphlets about folk medicine, mom's anatomy texts with sayings she'd written on the inside cover and a book on friendship from the early 1930s.

I couldn't let all that history go. But I did want to reduce the quantity. So, a friend and I created lists of books I would not keep: book title, year of publication, author. I then could sell or give them away. Just as with bookshelves, I can browse through these stapled lists any time. I see a title, I see the book in my mind, know what phase of life I was in when I read or bought it, whether it lived up to its promise or not.

The list lives in my computer as well, available as reference.

I did the same for vinyl records, mine and mother's, dating back to the 1940s and '50s. It wasn't that I wanted to get rid of the music, it was the bulky paraphernalia: turntables, woofers and tweeters, mid-range speakers.

Now on the list I can find an album I remember from childhood, or a favorite singer, long dead, go to YouTube, plug in the Bose speaker, and hear it again. *I Dreamt I Dwelled in Marble Halls*, Paul Robeson singing *Old Man River*, Marian Anderson with L*et Us Break Bread Together*, English music hall tunes, *I'm 'enery the Eigthth I Am, With Her Head Tucked Underneath Her Arm*. Then more contemporary favorites: those three sexy Italian tenors in their first Christmas show, YoYoMa breaking my heart with Dvorak's *Largo* from New World Symphony. Problem solved.

Still, the book problem persists. I didn't stop buying books after the first extinction. Then, as we moved twice more, trying to find a location that fit us, there was a slow-rolling Second Extinction, more lists. This didn't stop a new accumulation, either, any more than the erosion of volcanic deposits prevents new soil from being deposited on top of it.

Many of my favorite books are what used to be called coffee table books. Somehow coffee tables became "cocktail tables," then morphed into the current "low tables." Mine, by any name, continues to accumulate gigantic volumes called *Gothic* and *Romanesque, Wild Beauty* (old photos of the Columbia River from a Portland Art Museum exhibit), *The Shell: Five*

Hundred Million Years of Inspired Design, and Penelope Hobhouse's *Story of Gardening*.

More easily-read volumes live in my office, the living room, the bedroom, wherever a horizontal space exists.

In the Third Extinction, I began to read library books digitally while donating "real books" to friends. New rules: if it can be found on Google, don't keep a travel book. Ditto with history and political commentary. Never get rid of books written by friends. Know which books you will return to for reference and keep them. Buy a book if you intend to study it.

Still, the answer to the question how much is enough, with books and music, is easy and exuberant. Music and books: never too much or too many. As with sunshine and honeybees, grandchildren and chocolate, the word "enough" doesn't exist. There's always room in the house and the heart for more.

Things: A Practical Guide

At a certain stage Things begin to keep you, not the other way around.

Multiple voluntary downsizings have led me to find ways of dealing with Things. They may be the most pressing items for many people who wonder *How much is enough?*

• If you can digitize it, do. That allows you to keep certain things, while not sacrificing space. Photos lead this list. And you know how I feel about lists of books and records. Then there are essays written but not published, manuscripts I probably never will do anything with and old newspaper articles.

• If you love it, keep it. Art work, blown glass pieces, lacquered bowls from Japan, the lace handkerchief my mother carried in her wedding, grandmother's silver tea pot, a burl of wood washed up on an Oregon beach, buffed and polished by my dad. An incised copper tea kettle given to my parents as a wedding gift. The abstract painting hanging over my bed.

• If you use it often, keep it, especially if it nests, like pots and pans and pottery bowls.

• Keep representatives of things you want to see. For me, this is a pretty big category. I love interesting rocks. I've kept some obsidian, Biggs picture jasper, a large amethyst cluster my father found near the Oregon coast. A pretty rose quartz and a bold orange calcite, a small bit of Pele's lava from the Big Island, where the earth is still being formed. The original collection was much larger.

Ditto for unusual, small sea shells from all over the world, now piled in two delicate baskets instead of being spread for individual viewing.

I've kept two sets of porcelain dishware (one for Christmas), one of silver flatware, lots of extra serving pieces for festive dinners. I love them and use them, so they're two-furs—plus they represent others I've given to daughters, so they really hit three categories. Books go here as well. If I'd kept them all, I'd have no room for the kitchen! The one's I've kept represent stages in my life.

• Clothing: be honest. If someone else can use it, give it away. Ditto linens—for bed, bath or beyond. Also shoes. Be ruthless., you will buy more. Do not say, "I may wear it again." You won't.

You have enough.

A Certain Kind of Book

Oh, joy! Here near the end of a life enlivened by reading, I have met another woman who reads the kinds of books I do. She even lives near me. We meet, drink wine, talk. It makes me happy.

Before I met her, I had but one friend who read like that. He's younger, still climbs mountains and reads. Now I have two people to discuss a certain kind of book with. It is enough. Because some of these books only I will be interested in. I know that.

These books have footnotes. Or page after page of endnotes. They have nice, thick appendices. Sometimes the appendices and endnotes are a quarter the size of the book itself.

They have titles like *The Mind in the Cave, How Architecture Works, A History of Canada in Ten Maps* and *Sapiens: A Brief History of Humankind.*

Research, supported with authors' meaty opinions, form the beating heart of these books. It can be research about human nature (aka a biography or rarely memoir), about plant life, fungus, animal cultures or how the Polynesians sailed without compass or GPS.

These books are thick, and are best read in print because that way I can make notes in the margins, comments to myself, ideas that burble up while reading.

Lest you think I exaggerate, here is the unedited journal entry about one of those books the day I bought it.

> A new book purchased today. (Happy, Happy)
> Oh, great day—it has a Foreword, a Preface *and*
> an Introduction.

There's an Epilogue *and* an Afterword.
There are Endnotes, Acknowledgements *and* a
Glossary.
It contains maps. *And* photographs. *And* illustra-
tions. Lots of them. So many they have their own
two-page explanation at the end of the book.
All these wonderful things let me scope out the
book before I begin reading, help me get a sense of
what's in store as I set out on an adventure into a
subject I know virtually nothing about: navigating
the southern Pacific without instruments.

September, 2019
Hawaiki Rising: Hokule'a,
Nainoa Thompson,
and the Hawaiian Renaissance

Journaling

I've written to clarify my thinking practically forever. I began sustained journaling in mid-life when I was unhappy in my marriage and with my life in general.

I wrote to complain.
To whine.
To analyze.
To clarify my thinking—the old standby.
Journaling helped me move from one crisis to another—
I divorced and entered the upheaval of another marriage
     in another state…
a daughter struggled with alcoholism…
my father died…then my mother…
while working, I studied at night and earned a master's
     degree
another daughter fought Hodgkin's lymphoma and a
     vengeful husband…
the high-tech company laid me off…
we bought and moved to a third house…
I opened a business…
a third daughter was besieged by cerebral edema in
     Antarctica, recovered alone in New Zealand…
the tiny, premature daughter of another daughter
     successfully fought for life after her twin brother
     succumbed.

I continued writing through major decisions about retirement, where to live, how to set up these late, last years I hadn't planned to have, actually.

My life became placid—and I loved it. Now I had no crises, no emotional upheavals to write my way through.

How much journaling is enough, I wondered?

I read through half a lifetime of journals, volumes of spiral-bound brown covers and sturdy paper meant for painting or drawing. Instead, mine had blue ink scrawls to lead me through the years.

I culled a few ideas to keep.

I shredded the rest, thinking, *Who would care to read about my inner angst, these interior ups and downs?*

Then, too, as I read these volumes, the recurrence and similarity of my life issues astonished and eventually bored me. It told me, "This is enough. I'm finished."

Honesty demands that I mention, however, that there's a volume exactly like the shredded ones on my night table. I think of it as waiting in case I change my mind.

One must stay open to that possibility.

Random Travel Thoughts—A Recitation

I keep several small polished rocks on my desk and reach for one when my mind needs calming, or when I'm trying to think of something that eludes me. Most of them are the color of butterscotch.

I keep the names of places I've visited in my mind. There, where memories reside, the names become warm and smooth like the rocks. When I call upon them, the names release sights or sounds, sometimes even aromas.

To my surprise the beaches along the Mediterranean at Nice were not the lovely, soft, sugary sand I expected. My bare feet bruised on the rocks. Home again, I snuggled those feet deep into the fine, warm powdery sand of Arch Cape, Oregon.

The wind whipped my hair in the magic place where the Indian Ocean meets the Atlantic near the tip of South Africa. In Mexico I climbed the steps of Teotihuacán one fine hot day.

I wandered through the golden, art-filled rooms of the Hermitage in St. Petersburg, Russia, with awe similar to that I felt hiking in the solemn 300-feet tall aisles of rain forest on the Olympic Peninsula.

Florence, (both Italy and Oregon), and the Badlands of South Dakota.

I'm fond of strange, lonely places:

> Steens Mountain,
> Shiprock, Devil's Tower, the sandhills of Nebraska, and
> deserted Wyoming flatlands where long ago I watched herds of pronghorn antelope—hundreds at a time—run free.

Mile after empty mile of rose-, apricot- and peach-color sand dunes in the Namib desert of Namibia.

Stark, heart-achingly-flat Omaha Beach in Normandy.

A high mountain meadow on the shoulder of Mt. Adams in late summer where a miniature, rocky stream wanders through tiny, blue, red, yellow, white wildflower blossoms. Huckleberries on the way in.

The channeled scablands of Southeastern Washington, formed millions of years ago when Lake Missoula flooded again and again.

I've traveled to cities:

Paris, Amsterdam and Venice,
St. Petersburg,
Rome,
Amsterdam,
Prague,
Hong Kong, Taipei, and Seoul.
London, and Athens.

To islands:

Capri, Crete, Oahu, Kauai, the Big Island, Vancouver.

To both North America and Central America, a region of slippery borders:

Zihuantanejo (before cruise ships stopped there).
Lake Patzcuaro & Morelia, Mexico City and Puebla.
Banff & Lake Louise.

Anchorage, Fairbanks, north of the Arctic Circle. Denali.
A Japanese garden in Lethbridge, British Columbia, another in Portland, Oregon, near my home.

To Africa:

>Cape town, Windhoek, Etosha National Park, and
>Victoria Falls.

Are these enough?

I've neither seen:

>the Masai Mara nor
>climbed Kilimanjaro.

I've missed:

>Tibet, Machu Pichu and Buenos Aires—all of South
>America, in fact, along with Mainland China and Japan
>(except for one airport).

I've never seen:

>the Taj Mahal in moonlight.
>Gibraltar,
>or the bazaars of Morocco and Turkey.
>New Zealand.
>Never seen the "Holy Land" or Petra or climbed an
>Egyptian pyramid.

Should I try to see the Great Barrier Reef before it's gone?

>The Galapagos?
>What about Angkor Wat?
>I've neither swum in a cenote in Mexico nor
>stood under a waterfall in Hawaii.

But I have soaked my feet in snow-fed stream in the
Rocky Mountains of Colorado and slept on the shoulders of
glacier-clad mountains in Washington.

Pushing my body to its limit, I climbed to the summit of Mt. Hood. Then to the top of Mt. St. Helens, years before it blew up. And just after dawn trudged up one of those thousand-foot apricot sand dunes in the Namib.

Is that enough?

I've visited buildings:

> Georgia O'Keefe's home in Abiquiú,
> Fallingwater in Pennsylvania,
> The White House,
> The Tate (they were showing Picasso's sculptures),
> Giverney, with its gardens and pond (that would be Monet),
> Versailles and Notre Dame.
> The Grand Old Oprey (Minnie Pearl was still singing).
> The British Museum (so long ago I could run my hand reverently over the Rosetta Stone) and the Louve,
> (where Mona Lisa wasn't yet behind glass
> and Winged Victory became the most inspiring woman I ever saw),
> the Guggenheim (Wright again, a design he pioneered in San Francisco),
> The Museum of Anthropology in Mexico City (Aztec calendar) and
> a living rainfall (long gone) in the Royal BC museum in Victoria.

If I think about it just a moment, I remember the excitement, the visceral thrill of each one. They're embedded in my brain, accessible, waiting to fill me with joy. Are these rock-memories enough?

I think so.

Meander

I love a meander. Love the riches found, the unexpected gifts that appear when life doesn't go in a straight line.

Changes of direction have spiced my life—let's have a baby, yes I'd like to manage a group of twenty people even though I've never done it before, sure let's drive to Alaska.

Meander was a Greek god associated with a 250-mile-long river in what is now Turkey. His river left its high lake of origin, aimed one direction, found an irritant in the form of a boulder and some hard clay, so turned the other way, ambled along for a while, then changed direction again when something caught its attention or impeded it. Just so, it meandered to reach the Aegean Sea, full of enough twists and turns to give its name to posterity.

When stylized, the meander turned into a design now known as the Greek key. It acquired that name because Greeks used it on vases, in mosaics, everywhere. It's not really Greek though, it's human. We've used it on the cover since this book is one long meander.

Because it's made from one continuous line, the concepts of eternity, infinity and unbroken bonds of love and friendship have become attached. That may be an example of anthropologists and artists attaching their own meaning to what might have been pure design to its originators.

Meander speaks to me, just as he's spoken to an astonishing number of cultures for millennia. His meaning spoke well before his name, since the geometric, stylized form of the meander apparently has been around almost as long as we've been humans. The oldest example, and it looks lovely on Google, dates from the paleolithic period, or stone age, when it was carved onto a wide mammoth-tusk bracelet in Ukraine. That would be about 23,000 B.C.E.

After disappearing from preserved decorative items for a while, the meander showed up again around 2600-2500 BCE in Egyptian tombs from the Fourth Dynasty. It's been found on ancient Chinese sculptures of approximately the same date. The Chinese called a more flowing version of the key Rolling Thunder, a welcome harbinger of rain. It comes up again in Mayan buildings from 900 BCE, as well as in other Central American cultures. Add Indian temples, ancient Celts and Norse artifacts, Peruvian, Japanese, Persian and Native American textiles. That's an amazing sweep of cultures, history and geography for one design to span.

I knew none of this when, as a twenty-one-year-old, I chose the design both for my sterling flatware and my "china." What I did know is I loved the geometric flow of the stylized meander in gold on cream Lenox porcelain. The silver was an early (1913) Gorham design. They called it Etruscan.

My favorite conversations are meanders. One topic leads to another, which goes in a different direction until it, too, veers off, perhaps to return, but maybe not. Each turn or oxbow in the exchange holds the possibility of new revelations, facts or insights.. There's a comfort, too, in meandering talks. Time slows, becomes less important. New ideas can be born in such easy conversations.

Meander can give us the fun of discovery in writing as well, although current style discourages it. "Put the body on page one," mystery writers learn. "The first paragraph must contain the main point," journalists are taught. But beginning your story in an unlikely spot, high in the hills, following it downhill to the broad, flat meadow, letting it meander, is a slower, calmer way to develop the arc of a good essay, novel or mystery.

The Greek key, the meander, is a line with no beginning and no end. I expect conversationalists and writers need to apply it judiciously.

How do we know when a meander becomes enough?

When eyes glaze or readers fall asleep.

Holidays

Most holidays irritate me, with their trumped-up commercial exhortations to decorate (Halloween), spend money (Valentine's Day), cook certain foods (St. Patrick's Day), celebrate another country's nearly forgotten battle (Cinco de Mayo), or go somewhere to party until after midnight (NY Eve).

Except for Thanksgiving and Memorial Day, that is. Those two still seem to remain pure, with not many expectations for decorating or gift-giving. You cook a turkey for Thanksgiving and raise a flag on Memorial Day, and that's about it. No one expects much more. Veterans Day and Labor Day also have managed to escape some of the folderol of more colorful holidays. And who doesn't love a parade?

I used to think my aversion to holidays related to these expectations for activity, decoration and special food. As a middle-class woman of a certain age, I always felt society pushing me to create May baskets, to buy cards or bouquets, or flag-laden napkins, glasses, plates and fireworks, to stack corn stalks or pumpkins by my front door. Now, with a more mature level of thinking, I understand it's the expectations for an emotional response-on-demand that I don't like.

Take Mother's Day for example (it's an easy one). I loved, appreciated and tried to support my mother during her life. At the close of her life, my two oldest daughters and I flew to her home and cared for her. It was a good way to finish the longest relationship I ever had. Our tie was real and deep, the caring mutual.

But in most of the years before her death, did I send flowers or gifts or cards on Mother's Day? No. Did I feel pressured by contemporary culture to do so and guilt for not? Yes, of course.

Same for Father's Day.

Do I feel my relationship with my daughters has anything to do with whether they send flowers or chocolates to me on Mother's Day? Not at all. I love them, they love me, we talk when we want to or when it's necessary, we visit almost enough. Most importantly, I think we understand each other's lives and the demands they include. Expressing our mutual feelings once a year on an arbitrary day doesn't figure into the equation.

Sappy sentimentality can be a socially sanctioned way to avoid the hard actions required to show love.

On the other hand, I confess to needing a calendar reminder for all birthdays except my own. The fact that I know and celebrate my own day of birth is a reminder that, while people may ignore Halloween or Cinque de Mayo, St. Patrick's Day or the solstices, everyone wants their birthday remembered. Honestly, most of us want to be remembered on the day it occurs.

This, however, has not been my forte. I therefore invented the concept of "traveling birthdays." It's a (mostly) shameless way to cover a faulty memory and/or preoccupation with other parts of life, say writing a book, or performing a job, or traveling. It means you have a week on either side of a birthday to mention it to the birthday person. You can bake a cake together if they're little, go to lunch if they're your age, settle for a quick salute on whatever social media you share. I'm grateful these days to Google, who reminds me (over and over) about birthdays.

Still, I'd prefer to celebrate relationships organically, not tied to the artificiality of a calendar. I may not remember your birthday, but if I know you love daffodils, I'll think of you and bring you some when they show up in the local flower market. I'll call you for lunch when I want to visit, I'll be there to listen when you need an ear. But will I send you shamrocks on St. Paddy's Day? Or chocolate eggs at Easter? Nope. Not if you're older than six. My life doesn't run on calendar time, and I've never been able to make it do so, although lord knows, I've tried.

If you lump major and minor holidays together, ignore most holidays particular to one religion or another, if you ignore all "_____ history month" dates, you still have nearly twenty holidays to celebrate in a year.

Seems to me, that's more than enough.

Being Wealthy

Our big country contains many different cultures and they've long fascinated me.

I first thought about it seriously during an auto trip to the South from my Nebraska-Midwest home in the mid-1950s. With my husband on the way to an army base in Georgia, we watched as farms changed from the tidy, painted, fenced holdings of the children of German and Scandinavian immigrants to unpainted buildings with old bathtubs in the yard. When we arrived at Ft. Benning, the base was not segregated, but surrounding cities and towns were. Drinking fountains and store entrances were marked "colored" or "whites only." A local resident yelled at me one day as I started through a wrong door. Clearly we had entered another culture.

Some thirty years later, working in a corporation, I came to understand that men and women are reared in different cultures. It's one reason they have trouble working together.

Several of the cultures the country is trying to deal with now are based on sexuality—gay, lesbian, trans, bi, etc.—while others are geographical and/or historical. I think of the super-rich as just another culture I don't belong to, and thus find it interesting. In terms of this book, I find myself wondering how these people deal with the question about enough. Or whether it even occurs to them.

We really can't imagine it, we who are not stunningly wealthy.

His and hers private jets, or maybe helicopters, taking spouses to lunches or meetings at different locations in the city as casually as I might say, "Do you need the car today? I have a lunch scheduled." While many of us drive, bike or stroll, the super-rich make a phone call, a driver appears, takes them to the helicopter, and off they go. They descend to the top of a skyscraper, are met there and escorted to lunch with someone whose private jet brought them from London hours earlier.

A twenty-thousand-square-foot beach "cottage" somewhere in the world that's private. It has an infinity pool over the ocean view, an outdoor pavilion with dining accommodations for a dozen, plus a full kitchen for the chef. There are tennis courts, a row of guest cottages, a helipad and, of course, quarters for staff somewhere out of sight. Oh, and a gym, wine cellar and media room.

Say, another ten-thousand-square feet of "ranch house" in the Tetons of the American West, or in the horse country of the South. Ski mobiles with maintenance staff in the former, horses with trainers and stable hands in the latter.

Maybe, too, an apartment in New York, Paris, or London or a villa atop a private Mediterranean island with a bay so the yacht can pull in easily. Maybe all of the above, plus a primary home located somewhere in the Northeast or California, depending on the location of the underlying business or family.

These homes will have two primary bedrooms and baths, each with an adjacent dressing room the size of my condo with floor-to-ceiling shelving, mirrors, tables and soft chairs. The bar (see below). Maybe a chandelier or two.

A nanny hired when *each* child is born. Captain and crew for the yacht, gardeners for the lawns, mechanics and people to wash, polish and drive the cars. A chef, of course—maybe with his own staff. Certainly with at least one kitchen of his own and a butler's pantry. The house itself will have a minimum of two kitchens, one for cooking, a second from which to serve the adjacent dining room. There will be bars, too, a small, elegant model in one of the fifteen-hundred-square-foot dressing rooms upstairs, another near the media room, one by the pool.

Personal maids or valets…what are they called now? Personal assistants? Staff? I don't know, but they exist, these people who pick up clothes from wherever they're washed or cleaned or pressed, deliver them to bedrooms and lay them out for that evening.

People to help with hair and makeup and bring a cup of coffee, a splash of white wine or a sip of single malt along with the cuff links.

Maintaining such property and supervising people takes work, so someone needs to be hired for that, too. Property managers, people supervisors, butlers, someone to put the house on the market and supervise the sale if you're tired of it and want something different.

And the big deal, if you're rich enough, is the super or gigayacht the length of a destroyer. It will contain swimming pools, helicopter ports, I-Max movie theaters, museum quality art work, a place for your small submarine, more staff than passengers. The New Yorker did a story about the "supers" recently, and even with all their pull couldn't find out who owns what. Think purchases by shell companies in accommodating island nations, think non-disclosure agreements for staff.

I read about these people sometimes, wonder about their lives. The gulf between those with great riches and the rest of humanity always has been huge and I see nothing in my reading of history or current affairs to think it will change.

In fact, there are more billionaires every year, and they are going to do something with their money.

So I meander back to my question *how much is enough?*

Does it—should it—depend on what you're accustomed to?

ᴄᴄᴄ

Changes – A Lifetime

I like change. Probably because learning new things energizes me, newness seldom frightens me. When you thrive on learning it works like that, I'm guessing. Or maybe I just have a short attention span.

Change can be fun and amazing, difficult and scary, for good or for evil. It's the one constant all people face, no matter how much control we attempt against it. It's part of what makes travel a hoot of joy—the sameness quotient reduces daily.

Not everyone embraces change. Some of my friends fight new technology, sputtering and fuming over changes they can't avoid. Travel wasn't fun for my father. My brother has lived in the same house for probably fifty years. He neither understands the phrase "smart TV" nor uses a "smart" phone.

The nature of change matters to my acceptance or rejection. Stuff like technology or home appliances or how we communicate simply is part of life, for me. Let's get on with it without wasting energy fussing.

But child-rearing, how we treat people in public spaces, political discourse, attitude toward history and science, whether we should be a theocracy instead of a democracy, the ongoing abortion fight—those changes reflect shifts in this country's value structure. I won't address them deeply here; I don't intend this to be a political book. But when thinking about change, everyone has an answer to how much is enough for them personally. We get to choose how we react.

Many changes are powered by technology, but not all. Here are a few of both.

Technology

Telephones: My telephone use began with a heavy black phone. It had a base connected to a receiver by a black curly cord. You picked up the receiver, put it to your ear, and heard a female voice say, "Number please." The operator physically rang the person or business whose number you gave her. Then dial phones severed that human connection by placing your call automatically. Soon even "long distance" calls became automated. Phones moved from the wall to the desk and came in colors other than black. Now, of course, they're in our pockets, purses or backpacks.

They combined with computers and multiplied change.

Computers: IBM built rooms with cooling systems for the gigantic early ones. Now they're on our desks, laps, and in our hands. Some people run their houses with them. Computers do everything but drive our cars, and sometimes they even do that. It's the future, we're told.

It's also the present. These computers mean encyclopedias at our fingertips and cameras with us always. They give us directions. We wear them on our wrists and call them watches.

The Internet: Here's a story for you. In 1956, in the California Bay Area, I had a friend with "clearance." He worked, tucked away in the trees above the Berkeley campus, in a mysterious place that housed a cyclotron. It was called the Rad Lab. Locals understood it had a lot to do with the atomic cloud hanging over the world after the Second World War.

One day, sitting on the grass at intermission during an outdoor Gilbert & Sullivan show, he told me about a new system to protect information by de-centralizing it.

He said they were creating a "net" for sharing data, facts, knowledge. It was a system something like a spider's web instead of a top-down structure. He said it would be virtually impossible to bring down.

"Sort of like when part of a brain keeps working even if another part is hurt," he said.

The project involved the military and universities, he said. They each wanted different things but worked together, just as the great scientific universities had helped with atomic bomb research. While the military wanted to safeguard information, the schools saw a way to share it, linking institutions efficiently and effectively. Both goals pushed this new idea.

"I think it will catch on and eventually spread," he said. "In fact, I think it's going to impact society a lot...eventually." He was right, of course. Today we call this thing the Internet.

It "impacts society a lot" in ways we don't understand yet. My friend would have been horrified at the social media explosion and its less savory consequences.

Household appliances: I missed the true "ice box" era, but my grandmother had a fridge with a big compressor on top. Now refrigerators are slim and lovely, dispensing filtered water and ice from the door. Some are drawer-sized. Mine has a little orange light that tells me when to change filters. People who can afford it have no trouble with *this* change. Nor with the ones that brought laundry and drying indoors and installed them into tidy machines that can wash and dry clothes while we sleep.

Correspondence was hand-written in attractive Palmer Penmanship loops on paper. It took days for the post office to get letters anywhere, weeks for overseas. Now we type on the run with our thumbs and call a short letter "text." Some of us still use email, although younger generations don't as much. Both texts and email are delivered instantly, and people expect responses instantly as well.

How much of that added pressure is enough?

From the non-technology side

Children: Before my era, children were meant to be seen but not heard. My pals and I were thought to be independent actors who could learn by doing, were allowed to make mistakes, given great freedom. When we had our children, many of us regarded them as secondary adjuncts to a marriage. We called them "kids," lighthearted and warm. Now many middle-class helicopter parents supervise 24/7 and plan their lives around their children's schedules. They think "kids" is dismissive—completely missing the lightness of it. In fact, from what I see, there's little light-heartedness in today's parenting. It looks, from the outside, like a dead-serious, goal-oriented project.

A lot of what I loved about my children was having fun with them. Laughing and joy. They became teens, of course, much harder to find the common ground of laughter, yet we occasionally did meet on that ground. Those moments were precious. I think they helped forge a bond that survived those teen years, survived illness and distance, and becomes closer each year. I'm more on the side of giggling with "kids" than supervising calendars and transportation for "children."

Values: In spite of the changes that impact every part of my life, I've never had to alter the values I first learned: Leave the campsite cleaner than you found it. Each individual life is of value. Treat everyone you encounter with respect. Don't whine. Try to live up to your potential. Be kind. Educate yourself about the world you live in. Try to expand your life, not contract it. Participate in civic activities. Hold up your end of things. Do not pick wildflowers. If you do, they will not make seeds, and the next travelers on your trail won't have flowers.

I like to think these values determine for me what change to adopt and what to resist. But I wonder—are they enough for a mega-complex world?

Good Grief! Another Decision!

This piece began as a light-hearted riff on a lifetime of decisions. I thought to chuckle with you about how much trouble I have making decisions. Caught between my desire to move quickly and my unhandy ability to see every nuance of every choice, most decisions become big deals for me.

Of course, there were the big ones: *I'm going to college, okay, what do I study? Do I marry? If so, what about children? If I work, what field? Do I continue working now that I have children? Is it time to buy a house? Do I want the new job offered at work? For whom do I vote?*

I fuss and stew over even small ones: *Sleep in or hit the deck running? What's for lunch? Do I need a haircut?* When other people are involved it's worse: *What kind of food do these guests like? Where should we meet? What should I wear? Do they all know about that? Should I mention this?*

Little daily decisions weigh me down and I'd love to arrange my life to minimize them. Occasionally I actually have done so. Take breakfast (oh, yes, please do take it!). So much easier when breakfast becomes steel-cut oatmeal with fruit, flax meal and cinnamon rather than "What do I want to eat this morning?" *Pancakes? Eggs? Scrambled, over easy? Avocado toast? A frittata? Meat, yes or no?*

These minute-by-minute choices occupy me, irritate me, puzzle me, slow me down.

Sometimes I get so tired of decisions that I envy people who buy into retirement homes. It drastically reduces the number of decisions to make. Someone else prepares a menu, sets times for exercise, directs the programs. (Note to self: You tried that and it didn't work for you, remember? It only *seems* easier.)

But here in the spring of 2022, I'm assaulted daily by pictures from Ukraine of women younger than my daughters deciding to abandon their towns, their homes and jobs, packing their children's toys and heading for another country to avoid death from shells aimed their way. When I think of their decisions *(I may never see my home again, what do I take with me? What clothing, medicine, will my children need? If my husband is killed fighting, how will I reconstruct my life?)*, mine take their proper, minor place.

I no longer feel light-hearted.

Once I've poked my nose into that rabbit-hole, it's hard not to continue. Such decisions are made not only in Ukraine, but in Myanmar, Syria, Yemen and Ethiopia, I remind myself. I honor them in my heart, these women and children who take the brunt of the trauma brought to them by the great male god War.

My mind moves closer to home and I think that in our rich country, awash in prosperity, many women need to decide whether to heat the house or feed their children, whether to fill the prescription or buy shoes. Others need to decide what to tell their young dark sons about dealing with white law enforcement people, school teachers and other authority figures. And those teachers need daily to decide whether to go to school where a deranged teen with a weapon of war might kill them and the children.

I live in the West. Our fire danger has increased year by dry year. I imagine a wall of fire bearing down on my house—what to take, what to leave? Have you ever been close to a forest fire, radiating heat and wind and destruction? It has nearly unlimited ability to kill, to move at will, to sear lives.

These decisions are the real ones, the ones that will influence lives. In this way, they're like the big choices you make early in life—consequential, long-lasting decisions with unintended consequences. Those are the decisions that matter, and most of them are long behind me.

Time to stop fussing about the little ones, time to put this irritation to rest in light of a wider perspective.

Enough.

Part Two

Life and Death In the Wild

Learning to handle a .22 in Nebraska as a youngster, I watched with elation followed by some faint disgust with myself as a bloody rabbit twitched its last on the dry road ahead of me. "Good aim," my brother said. Younger by three years and teaching me to shoot, he was tickled with my success on our first foray.

Tramping through rustling Nebraska autumn corn stubble, a pheasant—speckled russet, golds and browns, reddish eyepatch, white neck ring and exuberant striped tail—took flight in front of us. I was unexpectedly glad my dad's shotgun pellets missed it.

In Colorado my teen-age self shot a porcupine out of a tall pine tree. He'd been part of a small army of his fellows destroying trees by climbing to the top and eating their sweet new growth. "Great shot," the owner of the forest said. "It will keep that tree alive a little longer." But after the big body splatted at my feet on the dusty ground from twenty feet up, I didn't kill with a gun again.

With a rod, however, as an adult, I landed a silver steel-head on a silver Pacific as flat as a Nebraska cornfield. Over the years came another and then another of the fighting game fish from river banks or drift boats in sunshine, rain and sleet. I pulled sleek, fat Deschutes redsides and rainbow trout from their wild river homes until one day I didn't. It had become enough. I needed to leave all the shining beauties in the streams where they'd been born.

My cousin Jim was an outdoorsman—100-mile bicycle rides, triathlons into his 70s, scrambling over high plateaus to shoot mountain sheep and goats in Alaska and Scotland. A frontiersman in spirit. Fierce. A hunter.

He told me this story:

Hunting with a group of guys in eastern Oregon, he became separated from them while trailing a stag. He caught up with the animal as it grazed in a forest clearing. Through the trees, he saw the classic painting—magnificent, healthy animal, 6-point antlers, gleaming coat reflecting sunlight shafting through the trees, peacefully nibbling meadow grass.

Then, in silence, the stag raised his head to look straight at where Jim watched from tree cover, rifle on his shoulder.

"He saw me," Jim said. "I felt it."

For what seemed like a long time, neither stag nor hunter moved.

"I was looking at the most perfect shot I'd ever had." He smiled at the memory.

"I couldn't do it."

The hunter lowered his rife, turned his back, walked away and never again hunted deer.

Contributions

One morning's mail brought these appeals for attention and money:

The American Red Cross (wildfires)

Yosemite National Park (save the national parks)

The Salvation Army (local Thanksgiving meals)

Boys & Girls Clubs of America (the Rosebud reservation)

The Library Foundation (gifts matched to Dec. 31)

Doctors Without Borders (malnutrition in children)

Cedar Hills UCC Church (annual stewardship drive

Nestucca Valley Presbyterian Church (ditto)

A National Geographic catalogue (purchases donate a portion)

Oregon Food Bank (share the wealth)

We support some of those; others are shared donor-list solicitations.

Other days we hear from the Nature Conservancy, World Wildlife Foundation, Juvenile Diabetes Research Foundation, St. Jude's research hospital, Heifer project, Medical Teams International, Mercy Corps, Finca, Habitat for Humanity, cancer, heart and arthritis organizations.

We hear from the people who take care of children born with cleft palates, those who need hearing aids, or dental care, or food and shelter. The University of Nebraska, Lewis & Clark, and San Francisco Theological Seminary for undergrad and graduate degrees, plus two other local colleges we give to.

We judge these all worthy, but we are finite and must choose.

We divide the appeals into categories: education, wildlife and the environment, support for women, feeding people, health, church. We look up their ratings for efficient use of donated money.

While we've saved money not traveling during the pandemic, needs have grown.

How much is enough?

Pop Culture

I feel as if I'm in a hot air balloon, floating calmly over the scene, viewing the lighter, less important parts of popular culture from a distance, detached, not participating.

Some of these things occupy the minds and take the time of many people:

The Met Gala.

Andrea Boccelli.

That singer from Iceland who wore a swan dress somewhere.

Lin-Manuel Miranda's latest effort.

Ken Burns' newest documentary of an era I remember.

JLo, ARod, and people with abbreviated names, nicknames, as if they are our pals.

Nascar and golf tournaments.

I ignore movie people and films in general. Singers whose names mean nothing to me, along with almost all their contemporary music. (Except *Hallelujah*, of course, which is lovely, and everyone performs sooner or later.)

Most of television. It seems to me survivor reality shows are direct descendants of pro wrestling, which I think is still around. I don't watch either. I've never seen a Kardashian show, although it's impossible not to know their names, even floating in my balloon.

I ignore most professional sports teams, automobile and horse racing. I do not fill out those complicated forms at March Madness.

I can't keep up with it.

No, that's not right—I chose not to keep up. We all have our own pop culture, and I'm quite fond of mine.

Fred Astaire, his sister Adele, and Gene Kelly.

John Wayne & Clark Gable.

Liz Taylor & Burton and that big diamond.

Jazz, ala Dave Brubeck and George Shearing.

The three tenors.

British and French mystery shows, Nature, Nova and Antiques Roadshow.

Nebraska football, the Seahawks, major tennis tournaments and the World Series.

My version is enough for me.

Then there's the part of popular culture that's not light at all. Popular culture always reflects the values and standards of its era. My era reflected white faces, with many of the black ones created by greasepaint. (Al Jolson singing *Old Man River*.) The exceptions were jazz and classical music, including opera.

In my day there was one narrative, shared by "all," of what kind of a country we were. Now our country has many narratives, and like me ignoring much of pop culture, it's possible to tune out the ones you don't like.

I choose to ignore the shrill conspiracy theorists, just as they, watching Fox News and other outlets I don't know of, ignore the reality I live in. My reality includes seeing many peoples of the US who didn't make it into the "shared" narrative refusing to be ignored any longer. Gay and lesbian people have almost made it into our common narrative, but we remain uncomfortable with more fluid concepts. And truthfully, they pose public issues we don't seem capable of fixing, like shared restrooms and sports. We as humans seem flummoxed by situations requiring new solutions.

I see a country where immigrants aren't just from European countries, but from all over Asia, Mexico and South America. They are becoming Americans just as the Italians and Irish before them, but in different shades of skin color.

I see a country where targeted black men are not dying in secret any more, where cell phones document their deaths and Americans who want to see, can.

I see a country haltingly trying to figure out how to deal with the ongoing fallout of the national scar of our slave-owning history. And the fact that Europeans violently took the whole country from the people who lived here, then tried to stamp out their culture to boot.

As each sub-group becomes identified, asks for its rights, fights in public to be heard, a counter-narrative springs forth. Elements of pop culture support them both.

Fragmentation makes us more tribal. In the name of inclusiveness, we create less inclusion. We don't know how to overcome it. Maybe we lack the will. As we know, the center does not hold. Really, it's long gone, just a memory of people my age.

Popular culture has a benign, light aspect I ignore to no one's harm. I wonder what will happen to our lovely country if I (and we) ignore the other side. The one that exposes issues of morality, ethics and what kind of a country we want to be. Can we concoct another shared narrative for ourselves? Create one popular culture that speaks to most of us?

If we can, it may be enough.

Worries

Plastic bags in the ocean.
Carbon dioxide in the sky.
Trawler nets drowning dolphins…even the great whales.

Pesticides stopping bird's eggs in mid-growth.
Bees and bats dying, monarch butterflies disappearing.
Passenger pigeons long-gone, bald eagles saved for now.
What about condors, their ten-foot wingspan against a pale, high sky—saved or not?

White and brown and black children practicing active shooter drills in elementary schools. My generation did that, too. In the prairie country, we dove under our desks, practicing for the atomic bomb that might hit nearby. What changes in the human story? It's the same expectation of disaster we teach children.

Young black men shot while jogging, or taking the night air on their own front steps, a young, black woman, an emergency room technician, shot in her home "by mistake."

Still no amendment to the US constitution guaranteeing equal rights to any woman of any color.

Hate and guns abroad in the land.

Pornography no longer hidden but available like Coca Cola in a convenience store. The Big Lie embraced as a tactic, no longer morally repugnant.

A conversation is always dominated by the least mentally healthy member:

We cringe from this truth nationally, daily.

How much can we worry? How much anxiety can a conscientious person bear about the deep-seated, systemic issues this country contains? And our world?

Is that even the right question?

Maybe the real question should be: What will be the consequences if we don't worry about these things?

Born Female

It would take more room than exists in this little book to name and discuss the ways women throughout the world and throughout history have been and remain "less than," second-class citizens in human culture. Women, as I see it, constitute the great underclass, the supportive base upon which the temple of human culture, of civilization, of male domination is built.

It's a difficult subject to write about because of its complexity and ubiquity. I've tended to think about it in terms of the world of nature, although that's not very popular nowadays. The human family reminds me of the lion pride, where the female births cubs, nurses and teaches them, is responsible for much/most/all of the hunting, and then stands aside if the male comes along to enjoy her catch and take his nap. Not an exact analogy, but good enough.

Whether it's the overweening protectiveness of the Victorian era, the compulsory shrouding of the female figure in the desert tribes, or exposing the female body in a push-up bra and skimpy pants to sell merchandise, whether it's the righteous hysteria of anti-abortion thugs, genital mutilation, sex trafficking, or rape as an instrument of war, the theme is there to see:

Women's bodies are for the taking.

For using.

For domination under any guise, including religion.

Women must be protected from themselves.

Decision-making is male.

Religion constitutes a special irritant for me, since my vision involves a "personhood" approach to the spiritual side of life. This means I believe everyone should be seen and treated as a person, not simply as a male or female or one of the current alphabet list of sexual designations.

It's beyond me to understand why a person becomes defined to other people only by who they are sexually. Obviously, it's important to each individual. But why does it matter to others at all? What is the pertinence?

Our current society is set up on a binary system, which creates practical issues that must be settled if we are to treat everyone as a person first, a sexual being second. But society is set up to deal with practicalities: Who goes to war? Who marries whom? How or why do you designate bathrooms? Who plays which sports? But spiritually? C'mon. We're human beings first.

Two of the three great desert religions claiming essentially the same god don't even allow men and women to worship that god together. All three at some level, legislate against women's ability to make decisions about themselves. The only way I can understand this is in terms of power. And fear. There's always fear in the background when power is asserted, no? What are men afraid of, that they must subjugate women?

But I digress. Let's take voting as a more benign example.

Just twelve years before I was born, women in the United States were allowed to vote as national policy for the first time. White men of property had been voting for a hundred and forty-four years. White men without property had been able to vote for sixty-four years. Fourteen years later, black men were given the vote. Although it was abrogated nearly at will in our Southern states, the national legal intent was there: Black men could join white men in the most basic rite of citizenship. This was *fifty years* before women.

All this history still makes me angry. I can see why a split developed between supporters of the Fifteenth Amendment and supporters of women's voting rights. Of course, racial inequality affecting former enslaved people and their children should have been rectified, and yet the fifteenth amendment continued our country's division into male (capable) and female (incapable) when black men gained their right to vote a half century before women of any color. Their maleness trumped all femaleness and gave them a right their wives and daughters and my mother still didn't have.

So the voting hierarchy established by law in this country is this, in order of importance:

White men who own property (1776).

White men of any sort (1856).

Black men (1870).

Women of any color (1920), except in the two final categories, whose treatment is a double disgrace.

The indigenous, or Native, population (1924).

Finally, Asians, (1952, the year I was a sophomore in college).

Let me be clear. As a woman, I'm very glad I live in the United States of America, a country founded on principles of the Enlightenment as viewed from a basically northern

European and English perspective. I don't apologize for that. I appreciate much about it.

We have the rule of reason and of law, a certain pragmatism about how far one will go to win, and a generalized belief in the basic worth of individual people. At least the law does.

We don't go in for blood feuds, we aren't terribly tribal, and honor killings aren't a basic value here. Women can be part of the work force, can interact daily with men we're not related to. We don't have to ask a man's permission to leave the house, we can drive cars, and we are at liberty to wear whatever flamboyant or suggestive or ugly clothing we desire with no need to cover it with head-to-toe blackness.

We control our own money, we own property, we have credit cards and earn our own credit. We go to school, all the way up to the doctorate level if we desire and can afford it. We are as free as women ever have been (as far as we know), and control our own lives to an extraordinary degree if we choose to.

We view ourselves as valid whether or not we marry and if we do, we can choose to keep our inherited name. Depending on our religious preference—which we also get to decide on—many of us are free to choose when and whether to have children. Some of us can make that choice even after conception has occurred. Fewer now have that right than when I first wrote that sentence.

Having said that, we need to acknowledge that many of those liberties are recent as human history goes. Others, such as equal pay for equal work, remain myths.

(Necessary addendum: We are in a period now where many of these basic concepts are under attack, not for the first time in the history of the Republic. But I'm writing this piece as if some return to basic values will occur.)

These examples are not equal, are they? Having your clitoris cut so you can't enjoy sex isn't of the same degree as having trouble establishing credit. Not being able to leave the house without a male is not the same as having to learn where in your city it's not safe to go running near dark. Not being able to go to school at all isn't the same as facing faculty preferences for male PhDs in tenured jobs. So why have I lumped them together? Because the common denominator is that those things happen to women and I am one.

Another list could be made of the ugly indignities men force upon each other, I know that. And I hope eventually human beings will take corrective action for both the women and men we oppress.

But I was born female and have been subjected to enough denigration for that reason and that reason only. I'm wearied by the casual assumption of male superiority that runs through so many of our institutions, public and private.

Enough is enough.

January, 2022

Death only removes a person from your presence. It
does nothing to disturb their place in your mind.
May 7, 2005

Expected: Friends die, pass away, kick the bucket…
their choice. The impact is soft, sad, quiet.

Unexpected: These cut sideways across your spirit
with a quick, lasting jab.   April 2019

At a certain age, you begin to think about death just as at
earlier stages of life you thought about getting an education,
child-rearing or how well the company was treating you. If
you tell me otherwise, I know you're fooling one of us.

I still send Christmas cards with a long letter to a number
of people. I care deeply about those folks and resolve not
to lose them completely. They reciprocate, and once a year,
briefly, we come close.

But when I don't hear back from them, or get an email
in return, I begin to wonder. Are they just late (some years
they are), are they not bothering this year (some years that's
true), or have they died?

Two weeks into this year I had one answer. A note from
an old friend's daughter, telling me her mom died early in
January. At ninety-two she'd decided against debilitating
cancer treatments.

That note came about three weeks after an email from a
high school classmate in southern California telling me her
husband died the weekend before. Heart and cancer both.

These two were the only high school classmates who married each other. I'd known the woman my entire life, the guy since junior high.

Then the dam broke. In short order emails and telephone calls told us we lost three more men who essentially just wore out, and a jazzy artist friend who'd concealed her age until her obit told us she was ninety-nine. All were friends from other years, other places. Finally, the youngest of the lot, a writer of talent, succumbed to her breast cancer.

Seven deaths to begin the new year. January, a deluge.

Each email, each phone call, bruised me a bit, diminished my life.

It was way more than enough.

🔗🔗🔗

A Great Love

The question in writing class this morning: For you, was there ever a great love? I work to define "great love."

I decide it is one worth wrestling your own demons for, one calling for strength instead of capitulation, needing clear-eyed reality, not only dreams.

In a great love, the two of you inhabit the same story and death will not change it.

Safety and excitement—I wanted them both. I knew they existed together. I sought them both. Knew I'd find them.

I wanted it all from love and found it.

It has been enough for nearly half a century.

June 10, 2016

War

You may think I shouldn't write about this topic since I've never been in the military, in a war zone, or in a country invaded. As with most Americans, I've been wrapped in security, living in the mightiest country in our world right now—probably the mightiest ever. The Roman army, after all didn't have atomic weapons, tanks or artillery. Nor could they sit at home and direct drones and airplanes to attack for them. No, I think "mightiest ever" would cover it.

Unlike the fish in the analogy, humans are aware of the "water" we swim in; we know the world that surrounds us. It affects us. So, I write of a long life, lived nearly constantly in the knowledge that somewhere in the world our sons were killing other women's sons—and being killed—in the eternal male battle called war.

In the "war to end all wars," my father, trained and ready, sat on his bunk in an East Coast army barracks, about to be sent to Europe to fight. The First World War ended then, in 1918, possibly saving his life and making mine possible. He also escaped the flu that killed many of the men on nearby bunks.

When the second world war began for the US in 1941, I was in grade school. I participated in scrap drives, gathered goods to be sent to "our boys overseas," and warmed to patriotic songs and atmosphere. I learned to knit, making warm things for those same "boys." That war ended with two atomic bomb explosions in 1945.

As my friends and I were graduated from our small town, Midwestern high school four years later, in 1950, North Koreans invaded the South, and some of those friends were drafted to fight. Five years later, my new husband was sent to patrol the DMZ in bitter cold—but the fighting had stopped in 1953.

The Viet Nam war crept up on us. US military advisors began arriving as early as 1950 to help the French maintain control of the peninsula. We took over when they left and by ten years later we were thoroughly involved. Until 1975— some 25 years of escalation. This was an especially ugly conflict that tore apart families and generations in this country as well as in Viet Nam. Agent Orange, National Guard troops shooting student protesters at Kent State, other interventions in Southeast Asia—Cambodia, Thailand.

After that, we sent troops or bombed countries in Southeast Asia and the Middle East—Lebanon, 1982, Libya 1986, with the occasional excursion to Latin American regions— Dominican Republic, Bay of Pigs in Cuba, Bolivia (CIA). We invaded Granada in 1983, Panama in 1989-90, Haiti in 1994. The senior Bush president took us into what we called the "first Gulf War" in 1990-1 to liberate Kuwait.

Then the planes hit the towers in New York and we began the seemingly never-ending war in Afghanistan—from 2001 to the recent pullout twenty years later. That war took my grandson's leg and mobility when he stepped on an IED. Back to Iraq in 2003-11, back to Libya in 2011. Back to Iraq again in 2014 to now, to Syria, 2014 to now. And let's add Yemen, where a naval blockade and special forces raids are ongoing since 2015. And back to Libya in 2015 with airstrikes. It just goes on and on, the names thudding like jack boots on our consciousness.

These wars, and other skirmishes here and there I didn't name, have been in the background during my sheltered lifetime, contributing the knowledge that the US is not a peaceful land. We didn't stop with killing and isolating original people here, we apparently are willing to fight anyone, anywhere.

An Oregonian article about three years ago quoted Jimmy Carter as noting: "We have been at war more than 226 years. We have been at peace for about 16 years" since the Declaration of Independence in 1776.

Two caveats about war: Over centuries, the silver lining of armed conflict has been advances in medical technology. The same male urge to dominate other people has led them to try to dominate wounds, loss of limbs, everything it seems but psychological trauma. The "shellshock" of earlier times has been renamed PTSD, but remains to haunt generations of trained killers—sons, grandsons. Daughters.

The second caveat: Anyone who lived through WWII must deal with the concept of a "just war." I believe that was one. Jews and the Roma people and dissidents died by the millions in the camps. If nothing else justified putting Hitler's group down like rabid animals, the camps justify that war.

Other methods of settling disputes have been invented, but none seems to catch the fancy of the old men who send young men to die.

And now, Ukraine.

卍卍卍

For An Instant We Know...

I think humans make the concept of god too complicated. I think it's simple.

I believe ordinary people sometimes catch a glimpse in our minds or spirit or consciousness of the connectedness of all things. Briefly we become part of the overarching web of life that includes all people, born and not yet born, flowers of the field and all animals, now and forever—in fact, all living things in the overarching context of non-living but formed universes.

I don't think you have to be a mystic to feel this. I've felt it. And I'm quite an ordinary person. For me it comes in solitude, and mostly outdoors, in a forest or on a flat prairie at night. Probably mystics stay aware more often or longer than ordinary mortals do. Or maybe they work harder to make it happen. Because it's my experience that these intimations of harmony don't last. They come unbidden and leave after dropping their astonishing awareness on us.

In these flashes of insight, we feel oneness, harmony, running from algae to anteaters, from orcas to owls, from raindrops to oceans, from seeds to needles to rainforest canopies. We know we always will be included in this extraordinary yet commonplace congruence.

I think that feeling, that knowing, that recognition of the singularity of it all is what has been named god. It brings a calmness and certainty, this feeling, and we don't want to let it go. If you've experienced it, it's changed you.

The knowing means we've become awake to the way we could feel in connection to our world and whatever lies beyond. For an instant, we know this feeling is the way things should be, that there's a right way for our world to be. We've felt it for a moment and want more. So we give it a name to try to hold on. We call it God, Enlightenment, Allah or the unspeakable name we translate as Yahweh.

What's wrong with giving this understanding a name and creating ways to honor it? Because somewhere along the line the word itself became personified and codified. It turned into various religions, with origin stories, pomp and its trappings, hero's journeys, gold, frankincense and myrrh. Humans can't keep things simple. And of course, power always enters the picture. Religions organized this oneness into hierarchical form—its very opposite.

Along with unnamed people through the ages I have felt it and understood it in my bones and know it's real. Briefly I understand that all peoples can—and should—live our lives in touch with it.

I think that's all it is, really. Perhaps this moment of insight, this glimpse of the ineffable, is enough.

Never Enough

Then at the end,

Of what can we never have enough?

What calls for

neither control

nor discipline

nor counting

but unthinking exuberance?

• Grandchildren. Never enough...growing, maturing, developing...still checking me out alertly, still offering honest-to-goodness hugs, still promising surprise.

• Daughters. I had three, added one. Love that they're all interesting, strong and we never, ever run out of conversation. Often into the nighttime hours...

• Stars in a dark night sky. Preferably viewed lying on my back in a field of pokey plants on a warm evening.

• Books. For heaven's sake, of course, books. Mostly memoir and non-fiction. Plus music. (They are together in my mind, books and music.) My preference is European classical, the three Bs, Tchaikovsky, Chopin, Dvorak, plus some opera. But then there's always Dave Brubeck, John Coltrane and—oh, yes—Johnny Cash. To say nothing of Neil Diamond. Eclectic music taste of a certain period. It's a little harder to enjoy hip-hop.

• Strawberries. Not wooden, designed-to-travel berries, but smaller, softer, alive-in-your-mouth ones. Oregon berries, the early Hoods, Shuksans.

• Laughter. Sudden, mouth-open, loud laughter. The kind that makes other people in the restaurant or bookstore or grocery turn to stare at you with faint disapproval.

• Curling my body around the warm, sturdy back of my love.

• Friends. The real ones who regard you, faults and all, without critique.

For some things, there's never enough.

Writing

Writing is a slow process—my mind races ahead of
my pen, or even my computer. I'm down the road and
rounding the bend with my thinking before my pen has
finished saddling up.

Sunday 4-15-83

Writing, what an old-fashioned word. Nowadays companies call it "creating content," an accurate but boring
description, like most corporate-speak. Especially in the
tech sector, writers are called "content providers," another
bloodless phrase.

Well, I've been both a content provider and a writer, and
I can tell you writing is more fun. Creating content uses only
your left brain, the executive, the editor who takes facts and
rearranges them into sentences. Directions on how to put
the crib or the motherboard or the submarine together. No
drama there, no tears or fear, excitement or the flash of recognition. These belong to writers.

Content providers often write to one segment and call it
their "audience," causing them to miss the mark. Writers,
great or indifferent, deal with the real world where people—
rich, poor, black or white, educated or not—experience the
same emotions. They are twisted into different patterns, but
are alike at the core. Writers know that.

Those emotions, combined with outside factors, can be
turned into courage or cowardice, rage or calm, competence
or failure. In the hands of a writer, as in life itself, they can
produce repugnance or a surge of warmth for a character,

revulsion or understanding, a nod of recognition or the surprise of unexpectedness.

These are the emotions writers can inspire in readers, something a content provider can't aspire to.

Writing, at least the part you might consider creative, is a come-and-go thing. I think it rises from boredom for me. Maybe that's not the right word. It's the space created when the house is tidy, the food pantry stocked, the monthly financial visit with Quicken over, when there's no one on the calendar, no meeting to attend, no reading to involve me, my correspondence is up to date, that my mind is free enough to roam at will.

Sometimes it's the space created when *enough* of those things are done, and I'm bored with what's remaining in the world of administrative detail.

Either way, my mind jumps track. It begins its own life of ideas and feelings and I know writing's going to be easy for a while.

I can write at any time. I know it truly is ninety-eight percent perspiration and two percent inspiration. Any newspaper reporter will tell you the same. But I also recognize those magical times when ideas and words flow instead of being hacked out laboriously one by one.

Remember as a kid on a bicycle, when the road was straight and you took your feet off the pedals and flew along, wind in your hair? When it's good, writing is like that for me.

Of course, any activity you get into with gusto has its moments of free-flow. It's called being in the zone and most people will recognize it. Time stops. When it's all working, nothing exists but the moment. Carpentry, cooking, painting, sculpture, surgery.

The periods of creativity I'm discussing last longer and come from nowhere. They stop as abruptly as they begin. So, when I recognize my mind is racing with delicious words falling into place easily, many of those administrative details go by the wayside while jotted words fall like petals in the wind on the backs of envelopes, writing pads, the "notes" app on my phone, and computer files. I get up in the middle of the night to note an idea or phrase. Later, the left brain will have to cut, trim, edit and polish, but for now, I'll write.

I'm not going to tell you I began writing as a toddler. I didn't. But I did read as soon as I could and never stopped. That's where it begins. By high school, I was writing news stories for the school paper, and became editor my senior year. On to the university, where again I was editor of the daily paper by my senior year.

After graduation, I worked in a newsroom, unusual for a woman at the time.

Every job I held found me writing part time. News reports for non-profits, speeches for VPs and booklets for trips to the Far East in high tech.

Then on to my own writing publishing business. A wonderful chance to help others and entertain myself. Toward the end, I wrote my first book, a how-to for starting and running a one-person business.

There's no real retirement for a writer. In workshops with an Irish poet, a sprite with a connection to other worlds, I found my métier—short pieces we called "miniatures."

The first book of miniatures was a chapbook. It was handmade, as they must be, with the help of an artist friend and my husband, the technician. It expanded into a "real" book, filled with highly personal bits that somehow seemed universal to my readers. A second book of miniatures followed, and this is the third.

These miniatures are longer, some couldn't even be called that. They're an evolution, which writing should flow into.

The meander has no beginning and no end, so perhaps it's a fit metaphor for writing.

For now, this is enough.

The End

୮୮୮

For Discussion Groups or Book Clubs

Readers of Sally's books report engaging in an internal dialogue with her writing. No surprise there, since her work is sprinkled with questions and observations. "Enough" also offers a sweeping view of topics and events of our time as experienced by the author. Many of us have lived through similar experiences. We probably will have different reactions.

This makes Petersen's books good material for discussion groups and book clubs. Earlier books have been successfully used this way.

Below are some suggestions for ways to begin discussions on topics raised by the book and individual essays.

1. The topics Petersen looks at range from inconsequential to serious, from light-hearted to heavy-hearted. Is this range one of the "meanders" she refers to? How does this contrast in the same book work for you?

2. Petersen's work illustrates the maxim that the most personal is the most universal. Which of her themes spoke loudest to you at your current stage of life? Which, if any, missed your interests completely?

3. An unspoken but clear secondary theme in this book is aging. Petersen explores random examples of how the aging process relates to what we do and what we pay attention to. She has some answers (Books, Things, Journals), but seems to have more questions as she navigates the back end of a long life. Does that resonate with you? In what way?

4. In Part One, the author deals with every day issues—what to wear, cook, when to exercise, downsize, etc. Which of these speak to your situation now? Are they issues of aging? Or just of growing up?

5. Petersen seems to want to simplify the concept of God into a transcendent experience open to all people. In her vision, this would not lead to religion—a structure, dogma, hierarchy. Do you think this is possible? Or is this just a dreamy, wishful idea of hers?

6. War would seem to be a thing, like great poverty or great wealth, that separates those involved from those not directly involved. But Petersen argues we all are impacted at some level by the American habit of going to war. Have you been personally impacted by a war? How?

7. Petersen finds many things to worry about. Her essay on the subject doesn't offer a solution—what have you considered? What do you do with the heavy bombardment of issues we face in the country and world today?

8. In the essay called "Changes," the author seems interested in how we decide what change to follow or adopt, and what to resist. But she really doesn't give an answer. How do you decide your attitude when faced with changes? How does it matter what kinds of changes they are? How do our values impact our attitude towards changes?

ℙℙ Petersen Publications
www.petersenpublications.com

$12.95

ISBN 979-8-9859679-0-6

51295

9 798985 967906